# DEDICATION

*Thanks to family, friends,*

*colleagues, coaches, and mentors*

*whose influence positioned me*

*to compete and win.*

*Thanks to colleagues*

*whose narratives lend*

*additional perspectives on*

*positioning and branding.*

*They're all star players*

*in my book.*

# CONTENTS

# FORWARD
by Tony Buchsbaum

What I know about team sports might fill the space between any two words in this sentence. So when the conversation turns to position playing, what I think of is marketing. I think about how brands define themselves in the marketplace. What I mean is, I literally think of a market, a huge open-air place where vendors compete for my attention, where all they want is a bit of validation and some sales. Okay, maybe just sales. But you get my point.

I've been a copywriter for 30 years, which means I've been a strategist for 30 years. And believe me, the latter is much more important. Why?

Well, that's the question.

Why does a brand matter? What product or service are they selling? Who could it matter to? When might the customer need it?

Strategy: the who, what, when, where, and why. Without those, it's next to impossible to market anything with real effectiveness.

Think of light bulbs. What makes one better than another? How much brightness will it give off? How long will it last? Is it more economical?

Or a new phone. How is it better than everything out there now? What's the cost? Why should I switch from an established brand to this one?

Coke or Pepsi?

Apple or Microsoft?

Advil or Motrin?

Strategy is the thing that differentiates a brand from its competition. Strategy defines the brand. It places a product or service in a unique position in the marketplace. It's from that position—and through it—that the product finds its market...and with any luck, vice versa.

That's what this book is about.

It's also what its author is about. I've known Tom McManimon for almost 25 years. The day we met, I knew I had come face-to-face with a powerful force. I knew I had met a man who loves strategy, an art director who loves the power of words as much as I love the power of design. Tom is all about the art and copy because he's all about the position. He's all about what advantages a product has, and he searches for those advantages like a man crawling through a damp, dark cave looking for hidden veins of gold. Once he identifies them, he takes that raw material and molds ideas from it.

Tom knows about position players because he himself is one. He's spent his life and career becoming a man who stands apart from the crowd, a man who's always searching for the best position both professionally and personally. He's as devoted to his work as he is to his family.

I'm both lucky and proud to have him as my friend and colleague, and I'm just as proud that he's written such an important book, one that provides, swiftly and simply, the most basic foundation of effective, even powerful, marketing.

# We were Position Players

# CHAPTER 1

# Moving the sticks

IT WAS A CRISP, BRIGHT SATURDAY MORNING in early September, 1976. The day that was about to unfold would be exciting, exhilarating, challenging and life-shaping.

What was about to take place inside 100 yards of lined turf was, to many, simply a high school football game. But to me and my gridiron brothers, this was our moment!

Most of us had endured two straight seasons of sweat, tears, injury, frustration and flat-out failure. We lost many games over that period. In fact, we lost every game, nineteen straight. But somehow, none of us were defeated.

This season we had a new, highly touted coach to guide us. Coach "Chappy" Moore. He was recruited out of the Philadelphia Catholic league, where he won multiple championships. And surely, with him, we were on the road to one for ourselves. Sporting slick new uniforms, we brimmed with anticipation of the success that usually comes with the arrival of a new coach and a new season.

We were excited. As a team, we knew we were ready. Each of us had a job to do. Just moments from now, in this one game, months of preparation would be tested. Would we make the grade? Would we finally taste sweet victory?

As we gazed across the field at our opponents geared up in red and black, they looked bigger than all of us—even menacing. How could we compete against that? After all, we were not yet a mature team. We didn't spend time in the weight room building strength and bulking up. At first glance, we had to be one of the least-imposing teams in the league. Still, we had the power of focus.

As an entire team, we huddled in prayer, asking for blessings and expressing grace, humility and gratitude for being placed in this position.

The whistle blew. Game time.

I was the center—a key position player—so it was my job to deliver the ball every play, block, blow open holes for the runner and basically not make stupid mistakes. Over the next few hours, I would have my head handed to me over and over again by a beast seemingly twice my size. Yet still, I held my own.

Never fear, we had a plan. Our approach was to force our opponent to chase us all day long. We were fast and deceptive. Quickly, we were running end-arounds, sweeps, pitches left, pitches right and pulling guard traps. Even John Madden would have been impressed! We were moving the ball for first down after first down—"moving the sticks," as they say. Soon enough a touchdown came, and we were on our way.

But we were trailing as we trotted to the locker room at halftime. We still had work to do. A lot of work. I looked around at my teammates and saw confidence. I heard encouragement. This seemed odd to me. After all, we were losing. But this time it felt different. This time, we knew we had something. We had a game plan that made sense to us. And we had a coach who carved out a position for our team to compete and win. We just needed one more half to prove we could come out on top.

As I said, I was not the quarterback or the heralded running back. I was the center, hiking the ball at the start of every play, working to block defenders and carve open running lanes—all while getting slammed by the beast across from me. I loved it! As the second half progressed, the bleachers and border fencing filled with fans watching and cheering in anticipation of our first win in three years. They wanted it as much as we did. Well, almost.

With only minutes remaining, the score was close—14 to 15 in favor of the visitors. We had the ball. This was our moment. We had a ticking clock urging us along. And I believe we also had the luck of the Irish on our side. We were the Fighting Irish of Notre Dame High School.

With mere seconds left, our chance to win would come down to kicking a 40-yard field goal. In some high school circles, that distance is unheard of. But we knew our place-kicker had the leg. Up to now, we had played our game using speed and deception, and we were in a position to win. Why change now?

While setting up for the 40-yard field goal attempt, we knew our opponents would be keyed up to stop the kick and end the game with a single show of force. We decided to shout out a hard-count and never hike the ball. Of course, this strategy drew our opponent off sides and resulted in a 5-yard penalty.

We huddled back up and decided to try it a second time. Same play. Surely they wouldn't fall for it now.

We stepped into our positions along the line of scrimmage. Our quarterback shouted a hard-count once more and—

The other team jumped off-sides again!

The beast across from me lunged into my face and knocked me right on my ass. "They did it! They jumped off-sides again," I shouted. "Unbelievable!"

We moved ten yards closer to the goal post, ten yards closer to our goal. Moments later, our placekicker drilled what was now a 30-yard kick through the uprights. We won! We screamed, we hugged, we cried and we laughed with our gridiron brothers and fans and family in attendance.

That day, I experienced success with my teammates. We won because we worked together towards one goal. For all our differences, though, what we had in common was much more important. And instrumental.

We were position players.

## Notre Dame High School
Fighting Irish —1976 Varsity

*There's our '76 Varsity squad with me positioned in the back row, number 52.*

# CHAPTER 2

# Winning on a new kind of turf

MY HIGH SCHOOL FOOTBALL COACH WAS SMART and a quick study on talent and skillsets—his own players' as well as those of our competitors. He knew that if we were going to be successful, we would need to know our competition: their tendencies, their strengths and their weaknesses. That would reveal our strengths too and help position us each week to compete and win. Our coach built a varsity team of just 22 skilled position players. But what made us a force to be reckoned with was the strategic Position Player at the helm.

That season our team was crowned co-league champions and went on to compete for the NJ State championship.

As a young high school athlete, I couldn't yet see the rich, powerful meaning of "Position Player." Nor could I see how it would impact my life and career and greatly influence my measure of success in the years to come—including the success I would bring positioning my clients to succeed in the advertising and marketing field.

CREATING, COLLABORATING, AND WINNING ON A NEW KIND OF TURF. In my early years as a young artist and studio designer, I focused primarily on the mechanics of design, crafting the visual details of my work. It seemed the writers wrote the words and the art directors handled the layout, typography, art, photography and more. Mind you, this was long before computers swept into our creative suites and changed everything. Designers like me really had their hands full.

The creative process quickly evolved to an arrangement where the idea or concept sprang from free thinking between a writer and art director. Art directors and designers now thought more verbally while writers began to visualize the idea more. The impact of the creative team emerged. Clients began to express their problem or challenge to the creative folks who they now entrusted as marketing problem solvers—much more than simply wordsmiths or visual craftsmen. We were invited in to better understand our client's business. Beyond art and copy experts, we became strategic thinkers. We began to understand how powerful our work could be…and should be. What's more, our involvement became a critical step in the creation of successful, effective advertising.

Focus groups, surveys and market research became more relevant. This gathering of intelligence helped inform the choices and messaging of creative ideas. In short, research helped make our creative work smarter and more effective.
And, after all, that's the point.

The emergence and explosive growth of digital communications revealed (as a by-product) data—more detail about customers and prospect marketing. Data-based targeted marketing became the norm over old-school mass marketing. Understanding the target audience and its desires and purchase patterns helped agencies present and position brands in a more pointed, specific way, greatly improving their chances for success.

# CHAPTER 3

# Lead from a position of strength

FORWARD TO LATE 2011. At this time, I had been a brand expert and advertising creative director for more than 30 years now—a successful player in my field you might say.

Over my career, I've helped elevate many national and international brands and launch several start-up companies. We've been fortunate to be working with one of our most valued clients, Prudential Mortgage Capital Company since 2006, when we refreshed their brand and marketing programs with styling and impact consistent to the Prudential "rock" theme.

Now, our longstanding client challenged us to reinvent their brand appeal once more. They had been asked to adopt a new campaign that their parent company, Prudential, was poised to launch nationwide promoting the tagline: *Bring your challenges*. This campaign would gain wide exposure, beginning with airtime on the Super Bowl. Unfortunately, "Bring your challenges" was not a message they felt aligned well with the real estate financing business. Their customers were real estate agents nationwide seeking financing options for a broad scope of properties such as multi-family housing, apartments, hospitals, commercial complexes, and more.

Being put in a tough position, our client turned to us. They challenged our team to create an approach that capitalized on the styling of their parent company campaign, while delivering relevant messaging to their customers.

Our first step would not be about choosing colors, graphics, or even media. Step 1 was: come to know the players. We asked, what were their strengths? What gave them an advantage in the sales process? Where was the "more" or the "better than?" Were they better, sharper, or more experienced? How did they stack up in service? How strong was their portfolio? How could we position them to win?

Conducting a series of interviews with management and brokers revealed their agent teams length of service, experience, and exceptional qualifications. It was evident these folks knew what they were doing. Over time, they had seen the market dive and climb, deals shrink and expand, closings stall or reach settlement. Whatever the issue, they understood how to meet the challenge and get the deal done.

This would become their position of strength.

How we expressed and displayed this in their work was still our challenge. Remember, our client wanted a style akin to their corporate parent's new ad campaign—sporting deep rich blues and of course, the "rock" icon. They also needed customer benefits in the messaging, while presenting Prudential Mortgage Capital as category leaders.

We delivered three approaches to preview. Two matched the style of their Prudential corporate campaign. The third displayed its own style, yet "played well" alongside that campaign. They selected the unique styling of the third approach. Our positioning message for the new Prudential Mortgage Capital Company marketing stated: *We get it. Done.*

Our creative team included a writer, art director, creative director, and designer. Each were talented in their respective position, but it never mattered who penned the words or who sketched the graphics. This team talked, pondered, proposed, doodled and got to the heart of the creative solution together, as a team.

*Fully integrated campaign encompassing market research, brand positioning, tagline, website and interactive emails, corporate brochures and sales sheets, biography profiles, market data sheets, and a presentation folder.*

# CHAPTER 4

# Positioning: Identify your unique place to shine

SIMPLY PUT, BRAND POSITIONING takes a product, service, company, or person, defines its key benefits and what makes it unique, considers who would care to have it and presents it in the most impactful and meaningful way to its target in order to gain their favor.

These benefits and unique qualities are gathered in one place: the Positioning Statement. There are 6 components:

1. Product/Service/Company/Person
2. Category
3. Target Market(s) + Customer
4. Key Benefits(s)/Value Proposition
5. Reasons to believe
6. Competitive Analysis/Differentiation

You cannot effectively carve out a strong brand position until you find a unique place to shine. This is your best position to compete to win—to win the hearts, minds, wallets and loyalty of customers.

You can practice your skill with focus and determination. You can have a breakthrough product. You can even offer an innovative service. But what will truly elevate you and distinguish you from your competition is knowing the strengths, weaknesses and tendencies—yours and your competitors'. Learning these things—through observation and/or market research—can help you strategize a marketing approach that highlights your strengths—giving you your best chance for success.

Investigating these details can lead you to that breakthrough moment when your proverbial "light bulb" clicks on, revealing your Unique Selling Proposition (USP).

Your USP is not always best defined versus the competition. You get to it by comparing and contrasting, but it should seldom (if ever) reference the other guys. After all, you're marketing your product, not theirs.

The basic tenet of marketing is having something good to sell, something of unique value to someone else. That's critical. Once you have identified that, the next step is to make the best product. And if you're the product, then the best YOU. Whether your product is an item or a professional service, the better your product, the higher chance you have of selling it. And the higher your chance of achieving success.

But none of that matters if you haven't considered who would want your product. And beyond "who" is "why." Why would someone want your product or your skills?

Further, beyond "why" is "what will move the customer to choose you?" What will motivate a potential customer to buy? What will convert a potential customer into an actual one?

- What is the product?
- Who is the product for?
- Why would someone want it?
- What will move them to buy it?
- Where are your customers?

Knowing the answers to these questions gets you much closer to the sale. Mind you, I say closer because it doesn't yet close the deal.

Answer these questions well—and you're on your way to carving out your piece of the pie.

# CHAPTER 5

# Crafting your brand's position

JUST AS THE CREATIVE TEAM BRINGS GREATER PERSPECTIVE to creative ideation, the same holds true when crafting your brand position. There are always a YOU and a THEY to consider. Two sides.

Think of the YOU as your product, company or service—or yourself. In the best of worlds, this would represent your brand essence. Think of the THEY as your customer—the audience you want to impress and connect with. How well you understand and bring out the best in both will determine your measure of success. Meeting in the middle is where the magic happens.

This "middle" marks your position, your best place to succeed. X marks the spot!

**Where do you start?**

Step 1 is to spend time, energy and resources in developing your skillset, your area of expertise or your product offering. After all, you should perfect what you bring to the marketplace.

Back in the early '80s, the agency I worked for secured the Jaguar account. The agency brass suggested to Jaguar that we would spend the first year conducting research while Jaguar worked to improve their automobile. Imagine that. You land a new client, then tell them they need to improve their product before you create any advertising.

My bosses made that suggestion because they knew that the real key to connection lies in understanding your target audience—and how they relate (or will probably relate) to the product. Get to know what moves your audience, what inspires them, where their needs lie, what their expectations are and how you can help them. This thinking will help you improve your product, whatever it is.

The answers come from investigation. From networking. From digging. And then from digging deeper. You may have a lot to say and offer, but the greatest asset you can bring to any connection is unselfishness.

So get out there. Inquire. Listen. And learn.

## Hey, its competitive out there.

It sure is.

And that's why it's important to do things the right way.

Look at competition this way: There's another party vying for the same attention or goal that you are. We've all heard the phrases: heated competition, fierce competition or even friendly competition. But however you slice it, competition is competition. The whole world is competitive. You already know that; you may as well get used to it. After all, we spend our lives preparing our minds, bodies, spirits and souls to be the best we can be in order to position ourselves for opportunity when it presents itself. And you know what? Your competition is doing the same thing.

So is every company with something fresh, convenient or innovative to sell. Those companies—whether new or deeply experienced—begin by doing the work to define their brand strength, their culture, their value proposition and their unique offering(s). Then, with the help of expert marketing and advertising direction, they shape their message to appeal to customers they want to choose their brand and help grow their business.

Below is a simple formula to follow when building your brand's Positioning Statement:

**BRAND:** (product/company/person) **is the one** (product category) **that provides** (target customer) **with** (benefits/value proposition) **because** (reasons to believe) **unlike** (competitive differentiation).

Here's an example for my own company, StimulusBrand Communications.

---

*DIVERSITY, BREADTH, EXPERIENCE & ONE-STOP POSITION*
*StimulusBrand Communications is a small, award-winning branding and advertising firm that stimulates success for large corporations, professional services organizations and start-up companies by deploying a breadth of discovery, strategy and creativity across a range of branding and advertising design media, managed by its leader, Tom McManimon, with experience and talent unlike many other firms that specialize or focus on a singular expertise.*

---

It's a mouthful, yes—no one ever accused me of being concise!—and while it may not be sexy, clever or memorable, it's strategic. It articulates who StimulusBrand is, what we offer, what our strengths are, what our points of differentiation are and the space where we compete to win and succeed.

Remember, a position statement reflects your strategy. A positioning tagline, which is the expression of your positioning, can be clever, sexy, or emotional. Above all, you want it to be memorable.

Let's explore positioning taglines on page 26.

# BRAND:
(product/company/person)
### is the one
(product category)
### that provides
(target customer)
## *with*
(benefits/value proposition)
### because
(reasons to believe)
### unlike
(competitive differentiation)

## TAG. YOU'RE IT.

For more than half a century, savvy advertisers have attached a short statement to their ad messaging, usually with their logo. This "tagline" is usually a short, pithy phrase that's meant to express the key attribute or attitude about the brand, product or person. It's the umbrella remark you consciously or subconsciously remember when considering a purchase.

Some examples through the years. Can you name the company attached to the tagline?

- We bring good things to life. _____
- Just do it. _____
- Think different. _____
- Where's the beef? _____
- Got milk? _____
- The Uncola. _____
- A diamond is forever. _____
- Tastes great. Less filling. _____
- Take a licking and keeps on ticking. _____
- Melts in your mouth, not in your hands. _____
- When it absolutely, positively has to be there overnight. _____

There are so many more—hundreds—that we remember for the clever or exquisite advertising that brought them into our homes. These were effective because they captured a new place in consumers' minds and hearts, positioning their brand to win. The best part? Each delivered on customers' expectations.

Results:
1. GE 2. Nike 3. Apple 4. Wendy's 5. California Milk Processor Board 6. 7-UP 7. DeBeers 8. Miller Lite 9. Timex 10. M&Ms 11. FedEx

# A brand that exudes quality, creates an immediate association of quality.

Brand recognition can lead companies to succeed just as fast as the lack of brand recognition can lead to failure. Consumers tend to gain attachment to a particular brand based on visual and color perception alone.

**stimulusbrand**
advertising | design ▪ marketing

Read: www.stimulusbrand.com/news-articles/articles/color-branding
**www.stimulusbrand.com · Call Tom at 609.538.1126**

I recall in great detail a train ride to Manhattan for my very first job interview with Time magazine. The gentleman seated next to me was reviewing a pitch he was about to deliver to the 7-UP team where he would introduce the theme, The Uncola. When I mentioned I would soon begin my creative career, he shared his creative approach with me. You might say he was conducting an ad hoc focus group with me. I was fascinated. I wanted to slow down the train and not get to New York so quickly.

Later that day, I met with the VP of Ad Sales at Time. He was very informative and patient with me. Here I was fresh out of college with a degree in studio arts and drawing. What did I know about advertising sales? Still, the time he spent with me was eye opening.

My day started out with a very cool experience meeting the agency account director who shared his genius "Uncola" positioning with me. What made my day amazing was seeing the same account director on my train ride home. I posed the obvious question, "How did it go?" He replied, "Pretty good, pretty good, raised eyebrows, we shall see."

By the time I arrived home, I knew the advertising field was my calling.

# CHAPTER 6

# Position
# before execution

EARLY IN MY CAREER, I served two clients who understood the importance of defining brand positioning first—before developing creative approaches. This made a lasting impression on me—but more important, it made all the difference to their success.

### Case 1: Schlesinger Brothers Fine Luggage

Schlesinger Brothers manufactures high-end executive luggage, briefcases, attachés, bags and accessories crafted from the very best leathers.

Over the years, Schlesinger has earned a reputation for quality craftsmanship, value and customer loyalty. Their products are regarded among the very finest and command a high price.

Their two target audiences were high-end business luggage stores and executive professionals. One was more a business-to-business audience whom Schlesinger needed to stock their line. The other was a consumer audience whom Schlesinger wanted to drive to the stores to make purchases. Schlesinger knew they needed to appeal to the specialty shop owners for shelf space as much as they needed to create an awareness among discerning professionals.

Our tagline spoke to the emotional, rational and behavioral purchasing attributes of both audiences.

**Schlesinger.** *The only case that meets your standards.*

## Case 2: The David Sarnoff Research Center

The David Sarnoff Research Center functioned for decades as the research and development arm of RCA Laboratories, specializing in vision, video and semiconductor technology. Its Princeton, NJ, headquarters was the site of several historic developments, including color television, CMOS integrated circuit technology and electron microscopy.

After 47 years as a central research laboratory for its corporate owner RCA (and briefly for successor GE), in 1988 the David Sarnoff Research Center was transitioned to Sarnoff Corporation, a wholly owned subsidiary of SRI (Stanford Research Institute) International. SRI, though, had no need for two research centers. So now, for the first time, Sarnoff Corporation had to act like an independent and define its purpose, build its own identity, develop a business plan and market itself.

We took stock of the Sarnoff Center's history of innovation and aligned its experience to its new purpose. New advertising featured breakthrough innovations captioned with their associated years, including multiple Emmy awards. The lead ad of the new marketing campaign introduced a headline:— **"Still Crazy After All These Years"**—with the tagline *"Heads in the clouds. Feet on the ground."*

## Today's crowded marketing landscape.

Today we're exposed to more messages from more media sources than ever before. Print, direct mail, television, radio, video, web, outdoor, interactive, social media channels, mobile and many more delivery vehicles.

With all of that, what messages rise to the top? What breaks through? What do your customers remember and react to?

The truth is, it's getting harder to find our optimal target customer, and then break through and communicate just the right points that cause them to act. Given that landscape, the power of long, expressive taglines is over. Many advertisers don't even use taglines. Those that do typically display a short phrase or emotional attitude statement. Tags can sometimes be one or two words, three to four at most.

Some recent examples:
- Think small.
- Open Happiness.
- Zoom Zoom.
- The miracles of science.
- Taste the rainbow.
- Think Different.

**Here's a few tags created by StimulusBrand Communications.**

- *Collective wisdom. To your benefit.* This launched as a result of two corporate benefits companies merging and taking on the name of its new parent company, Brown & Brown. The phrase, for Brown & Brown Benefit Advisors, speaks to their experienced talent and range of employee benefits.

- *Know-how. To succeed.* This was developed for Academic Administrators Institute, a series of training programs for teachers and professionals.

- *We get it. Done.* This tag for Prudential Mortgage Capital Company highlights the staffing of long-time expert financing professionals and their exceptional track record for closing deals.

- *The room comes alive.* This tag was developed for Reid Sound, a group that outfits companies with sound systems and theatres, while also staging events such as graduations, concerts, and stage shows.

# CHAPTER 7

# Don't just take my word for it

I WAS MENTORED EARLY IN MY CAREER by a brilliant creative director who always seemed to come up with that "unexpected" approach. I used to wonder, "Who thinks like that?" and "What's going on inside his head?"

Then I realized it's all a matter of perspective. One look around the agency creative department and I knew there were all sorts of perspectives in one place, which I found exhilarating and fun—never dull for sure. The challenge was—and is, still—bringing something new to every assignment, a fresh perspective, a clever expression or striking photo. In short, new ideas.

Of course, having your own perspective is only half the equation. Understanding your target customer and what they think, feel and determine as important is the perspective that can help your precious idea break through.

Ask a politician, "what's your position on the issue?" and you may hear a strategically crafted reply or statement where they stand on a matter. This enables them to maintain a position of strength from which to operate. It is in this way that politicians are not just "players" but also, position players.

**I asked, "what's your position on positioning?"**

To offer additional perspectives, I asked a group of trusted colleagues and friends to share their thoughts and experiences: a former agency partner, a client, and two industry colleagues. The following pages feature a brief background and narrative from each of them. I am grateful to each for their contribution and their influence on me.

*Ron Wachino is accomplished at the highest level as an advertising copywriter and agency creative director. His work has elevated countless national and international brands to global prominence, while garnering him many of our industry's most prestigious awards. Ron was my first agency copywriter partner, and he showed me the value in creative thinking before execution. To this day, he knows how to turn a phrase that turns heads.*

"I'M A LOVER OF WORDS. A lover of ideas. Big, bold ones. My greatest satisfaction comes when I create something, or help someone else create something, that makes a difference. To my client's business, or to the world at large. I've led accounts. I've led new business pitches. I've led my dog Tucker past a Rottweiler that was up to no good. I've been in the ad business for, well, a long time. But I believe my best ideas are still ahead of me."

### My Position on Positioning.

"All brands who position themselves successfully do one thing very well. They buy a piece of land for their brand, and build something unique.

"The real estate analogy is fitting because, when you buy land, no one else can build on that land. It's yours. You paid for it. You have the deed. And, like real estate, you own what's above it and what's below it.

"But unlike real estate, there's no law that says how big your building can be. Or how high it can go. Very exciting indeed.

"Some marketers, though, in their infinite shrewdness, will try to buy property next to your land. And hope that, to a consumer, what they're building is similar to what you're building. And maybe it's even a little cheaper.

"Well, that's when you have to start building something else.

"Equity.

"And that starts by creating a voice that's different from your 'next door neighbor.' Your voice can be expressed as a certain attitude. Take Adidas, for example. Their voice is embodied in three words: Impossible is nothing. So, their brand—the 'house' they're building—is about attaining the unattainable. Pushing beyond what you always thought was your limit. Visceral. Gutsy.

"And, if reinforced with a constant stream of advertising which finds new and fresh ways to articulate that voice, the position they've staked out is clearly defined in the consumer's mind. And won't be confused with the athletic apparel company that tries to move in next door.

"So buy your land. Think about the voice that your product or service can most naturally adopt. What's believable? What's true? What's compelling? Do your diligence to make sure you're not encroaching on someone else's turf. Then turn your strategic and creative people loose on different ways to express that voice.

"And start building something."

*Prior to forming **Attractivate**, Kelly Stewart served as Director of Marketing for MMS Education, Inc., a media marketing services client of StimulusBrand Communications. Kelly and I continue to work together serving on the marketing committee to Notre Dame High School—our alma mater.*

"HELLO! I'M KELLY STEWART, an On-Demand Marketing Director, Speaker, Champion for Positive Businesses, and Practical Optimist. Through my company, **Attractivate**, I work closely with business owners and leaders helping them look through a positive lens to speak more authentically about their brands, create marketing strategies that build on what's working, and engage all of the people essential to their success. Our clients want to put purpose into their everyday business practices and succeed in the emerging for-benefit economy."

## *Purpose* as a Positioning Guidance System

"Every day, many people hop into cars and depend on the Global Positioning System to help them find their way to somewhere. The now-ubiquitous GPS is owned by the U.S. government and operated by the U.S. Air Force. It's a scientific system that relies on absolute location, relative movement, and time transfer to do its job. It navigates people around long and winding country roads, busy city streets, and suburban enclaves.

At some point or another most of us have followed GPS directions into some kind of unknown territory. Even people with highly developed internal compasses have done it. I know this because I'm the wife of one and the daughter of another. The GPS is effective and reliable in helping us get from where we are to where we want to be, and we follow its instructions because we trust in that purpose.

"When we talk about purpose in relationship to our brands, we can think of it in exactly the same way. Purpose is a Global Positioning System that helps us develop relationships with our stakeholders —also known as all of the people essential to our success. When people identify with our purpose, they trust us to get them from *where they are* to *where they want to be* because the company provides a desired or needed outcome such as a product or service, an exciting job opportunity, or a strategic partnership.

"Branding is global in that we all operate in an informed, connected, and transparent market. Whether operations are contained to one location or not is irrelevant. Our brands are accessible all over the increasingly congested yet high-speed information superhighway. From company-owned websites, through social media platforms, resource directories, review sites, and employment search engines, our stakeholders have ample and easy access to our brands. Today, the notion of a brand image that is projected to only one group of people, such as prospects, is nostalgic, not strategic. Our brands impact clients, employees, partners, vendors, bankers, investors, and the people in our physical neighborhoods and online communities. Today, there is only brand reality.

"Purpose is the ultimate positioning proclamation for our brands. To refer to it as a statement leaves out the *emotional tug* or other movement that an authentic purpose should elicit from the people essential to our success. Purpose is relevant to all who encounter it, regardless of the nature of their relationships with our companies. Using only a handful of carefully selected—and extremely meaningful words—it is, undoubtedly, the shortest story ever told about how the company creates value for others."

### Letting clarity lead the way

"This clarity of purpose helps companies become more resilient to on-going social, economic, technological, and environmental changes. How we create value for others in light of these circumstances may change; the products and services we offer will certainly evolve due to technological breakthroughs or marketplace competition to name two."

### Are you acting with purpose?

"Purpose is about why we do what we do. It acts as a guidance system, continually linking the company's values to the outcomes it creates for others, effectively and reliably positioning the company over the long term. It stands the test of time while allowing us to connect and resonate with people on the cognitive and emotional levels that help them make decisions.

"Whether wanting to buy a product or service that makes their lives easier, faster, or better, needing to find a job where they can flourish, or making an investment in a company they believe in, people are innately wired to move. In this context, the company's purpose ignites our enthusiasm for developing marketing and communications content, recruiting materials, and even contracts that speak directly to the wants and needs of others while inspiring confidence in our companies. When we do this, it helps others envision working with us (or for us) which alleviates the perception of risk people may have about taking the next step to work with us, or for us, or in some other way contribute to our success.

"Think about that for a moment. Highly successful companies have a stated purpose, a reason for being, and it rarely mentions making lots of money. When purpose reflects a genuine desire to do good for others while doing good for ourselves, and we align our communications and business practices to it, we are exceptionally positioned to earn our stakeholders' trust. And that's a worthwhile destination for every business."

*Mark Iorio is the founder and president of The Mega Group, a full-service branding and marketing consultancy in Hamilton, New Jersey. He is a high-level strategic thinker, motivator, mentor and active community leader. Always ahead of his time, his cutting-edge thinking regarding customer engagement and brand management have been the hallmarks of many successful client programs over the past three decades.*

*Anyone who has ever met Mark knows he is a true people person who is fully engaged in the moment. As Mark says, "There are constantly new and evolving ways to create and deliver your message. Knowing how to refine your story and possessing the ability to capitalize on all of the tools that are available makes you truly competitive."*

*I have known Mark for more than 20 years as a business colleague, competing agency leader, and as a friend. I am grateful to him for sharing his thoughts and expertise with you in this book.*

"THERE ARE FEW WATERSHED MOMENTS IN BUSINESS where one can point to a sea change in business planning and strategy. We are closing in on that time now with a new focus on internal branding communications programs."

## The shift from external marketing to internal marketing: What does it mean for your business?

"A transformational marketing shift is occurring in the business world. Slowly but surely companies are beginning to understand the importance of internal communication and employee education/motivation as a key driver of business results. Without an internal focus on delivering the right customer experience, executives are realizing that much of their external marketing dollars are wasted due to poor internal communications, brand positioning, and brand promise."

"Obviously, employees are a critical link in the customer experience. The good news is that the vast majority of employees want to be part of the vision for the company they work for. *Turning employees into brand advocates translates into better retention and a more highly motivated staff.* Companies find that spending time educating and motivating staff around their role in the overall brand, enables employees to come out of their silos and produce results that translate right to the bottom line."

## The value of brand advocates

"This is important because employees and other stakeholders will always be the most effective tool in the marketing communications arsenal. Word of mouth advertising will always be the most effective method of spreading the brand message. Effective internal and external communications programs are a delicate combination of art and science, which few corporations ever master. Communications programs need to be graphically pleasing, combine some level of psychology, and answer "the what's in it for me" question. Advertising is expensive for many firms and many who spend large sums of money on marketing have a difficult time calculating a credible ROI model, with much of the effort rendered ineffective."

"This begs a few questions:

- Should employees be expected to spread the good word over and above their stated role?
- Should we incentivize employees to become brand advocates?
- Are employees our strongest and most efficient resource to deliver our brand message?"

**Telling the money story**

"So with all this said, what is the money story that rationalizes this 'new shift' in the marketing mindset? It makes sense that internal communications campaigns need to be implemented, and with a recent Towers Watson study1 as our backdrop, it stands to reason that effective internal programs will yield a considerable return on shareholder value. In this era of unprecedented cuts in marketing budgets, how do we rationalize spending more money on new programs? The answer is that the money shift is transformational, it means budgets transfer, and it requires new thinking, education and selling. Corporations must use a portion of their allocated expenditures for internal brand building campaigns and more effective internal communications programs.

"The following survey from Canadian Marketing Association's Branding and Strategic Planning Council sheds some light on rationalizing a 'carved out marketplace' for internal communications."

**Are your internal branding efforts working?**

"To better understand the inner workings of internal branding within organizations, the Canadian Marketing Association's Branding and Strategic Planning Council surveyed marketers about their organization's internal branding activities, measures of effectiveness, and their personal involvement."

"Overall, 475 respondents representing a cross-section of industry sectors, business sizes, B2B, and B2C companies completed the online survey. Two questions were asked to gauge level of involvement with internal branding:
- Internal branding is the promotion of a company's brand values amongst its employees.
  - Does your company engage in internal branding?
  - Would you say you are personally involved in the development of internal branding initiatives?"

### Personally involved in internal branding?

"Overall, 284 marketers that are personally involved in internal branding were asked a series of questions focused on departmental involvement, dissemination of internal branding initiatives, spending, and measures of effectiveness.

"Development of internal branding strategies tends to be shared by the marketing group and executive team with more than one-quarter mentioning internal branding as a marketing responsibility and 72% saying the executive team holds some responsibility.

"External agencies are engaged by one-in-five companies surveyed."

### Marketing Viewed as Important, But Tactical

"The report also examined the perception of marketing by executives. While 82% percent of respondents agreed or strongly agreed that marketing is important to their company and 73% agreed or strongly agreed that marketing is the 'public face' of corporate strategy, only 37% of companies said they have a VP of marketing or a chief marketing officer. This is likely due to the perception that the marketing department carries out strategy, rather than develops it. This tactical perception of marketing was confirmed with 71% of the executives who responded either agreeing or strongly agreeing that marketing's primary function is to generate leads."

### Personal Viewpoint: Peter DeLegge

"Marketers would do well to heed the message of this study. That is, marketers must measure and illustrate the effectiveness of their initiatives in order to protect their budget and be perceived as strategic by the executive team. In short, marketing must prove its worth."

"The credibility gained through greater accountability and increased consistency with corporate strategy is likely to help move marketing up the strategic food chain of an organization. If the marketing department can prove it adds significant value in terms that the CFO and CEO (and consequently, the executive team) respect—that is, in terms related to the business strategy, and specifically, in financial terms or, at least, as measured through client acquisition, client retention, cross-selling, etc.—it is likely to significantly increase its odds of gaining a place at the executive table or, if it is already at the table, increase its influence.

"A number of organizations have made progress through greater collaboration between the marketing and finance departments. In many cases, it can make sense for these two departments to work together to establish metric standards and processes."

*"Especially in a difficult economy, greater accountability and processes for marketing expenditures not only result in more effective marketing programs, it increases both the budget's and the staff's odds of survival."*

### Making the case within your organization

"How can marketers get the airtime we need in corporate America to build a convincing story that internal communications leads to a greater shareholder return and greater overall awareness? By taking an analytical, bottom-line-oriented approach, we can make the case for internal communications and elevate the function to its proper role as a driver of business results.

As more data comes to light about the shift that is taking place, we can point to industry trends as further support. Either way, change is occurring now. New forums on internal branding are well attended, the speakers are getting better and the participating corporations are getting larger. The marketplace is primed, the interest is high, the shift is on and it's time for marketers to seize the opportunity."

**What does this mean?**

A member of the Branding and Strategic Council summarized his thoughts around the research findings as follows:

*"The comments and the statistical results suggest that there is still a big differential between those working in a company that would like to see the management 'walking the talk' and those who actually do have management that 'walk the talk.'*

*"The discrepancy between employees believing in their company's values (only 43% believe), and the company brand values themselves, suggests that the way companies organize themselves and do business do not reflect the aspirations and desires of the people who work in them.*

*"The low percentage (28%) who feel that they are rewarded for behaving consistently with their company's brand values, suggests that lip service only is paid to brand values.*

*"i.e. in reality the company promulgates amongst its employees other attributes of how to be successful. (Like contributing to the bottom line?) The incredibly low proportion (7%) of respondents who think their brand values provide guidance as to how to treat other employees suggests that brand values do not address human interrelationships in a meaningful way."*

– Hugh Oddie

### Why do internal communications matter?

"There is a clearly identifiable gap between the company brand (what we say) and the company culture (what we do). You don't need to look much further than your local bank, your favorite airline, retailer or grocery store. As consumers, we experience the letdown almost every day by walking into a retailer only to wait in line forever or be treated by a rude customer-care representative. How and why does this happen over and over again? It's because companies rarely take the time and have the discipline to teach and coach employees, management and staff how to deliver on the company's brand promise."

"I am not talking about the mission statement, which sits in the lobby and collects dust, or the company's value proposition, which employees read once in a while. I'm talking about an overall internal branding program that gets each and every employee on the same page regarding the company's brand promise or as my partner likes to put it, the 'Role Target.'

*As founder of The Presence Equation™ , Lisa Manyoky is a Presence and Communications Specialist to individuals and organizations.*

*As a career entrepreneur who is also a DiSC® trainer and a licensed, specialty-certified coach with a neuroscience focus (wow!), Lisa blends an understanding of brainpower, behavior, aesthetics and communication with business smarts to help professionals figure out what they want to do, get where they want to go and keep on keepin' on when change is uncomfortable. She is admittedly a Maverick, a firecracker who champions self-mastery, integrity, kindness and excellence. She is the consummate wordsmith with an energetic style, a quick wit and an expansive mindset.*

*Lisa's giant smile and enthusiasm have a way of grabbing attention, keeping interest and raising the energy in the room. She has also been a weekend warrior. Her work as a Mental Performance Coach to youth Ice Hockey teams helped players learn to use the muscle between their ears to improve performance.*

*I have known and collaborated with Lisa for several years. She is in her own right a Position Player. I am grateful to her for sharing her expertise and perspectives on brand positioning.*

"I HAD ALWAYS BEEN FASCINATED by what made some businesses take off fast, some stall and others, crash and burn. Solidly built brands didn't always work. Talented teams didn't always have the impact they sought. Well-crafted messaging didn't always capture attention. Access to all the technology in the world didn't guarantee profit.

And then, I took a seminar titled "The Neuroscience of Success." After only a few hours of listening, the fog lifted. I got it. Branding, teamwork and technology do generate business momentum, but science—neuroscience—explains why focus and connection are necessary to sustain it.

Consider this analogy. On its own, a paper clip is not naturally magnetic. But, if you rub it back and forth against a strong magnet, it becomes a magnet itself, and can pick up other paper clips to form a chain.

Why?

A paper clip is composed of tiny particles that each has its own magnetic field. Rubbing the paper clip against a magnet aligns these fields, pointing them all in one direction. As a result, their collective power increases—they can now form and hold new connections.

Go ahead, try it.

And so it is with position statements and position players. Both are mindset, behavior and performance unifiers that help businesses attract and secure a position in a market and, with continued alignment, anchor that position in ways that last."

### Where Positioning Begins

Simply put, when all of you or your business is moving in the same direction, you have more power. Where you decide to move starts in the brain.

The mind is a field of energy that is responsive to focus. It does not judge good or bad, right or wrong. Rather, it follows the lead of your attention, no matter what the object of your attention might be. With focus, brain circuitry activates, and chemicals release to form links. Over time and with repetition, these links align, stabilize and alter the structure of the brain. They create pathways that influence what you notice and what you don't.

Think for a minute about the purpose of blinders on a race-horse. The blinders eliminate distractions from other horses on the track and spectators in stands by keeping the horse focused on the goal ahead: the finish line. Chemical pathways in the brain do the same, which is why focusing on possibilities and all things positive is a critical component of accomplishment and success.

### How a Position Statement Works

While positioning measures your strengths and weaknesses and those of your competition and reveals your place to compete, a position statement functions like blinders. It blocks out interference, helps you "see" those you wish to serve, and provides guidelines for language that resonates with them. It also sets standards of universal performance that everyone in your business must uphold. Together, when they all align to support the positioning initiative, there's power, and lots of it.

The words of a position statement must be specific, deliberate and on point. Generalities, sweeping superlatives and crapshoot vocabulary leave room for interpretation, and in particular, mis-interpretation. That said, positioning is not a "lemming approach." -

It is not designed to suppress creativity or confine original thinkers. Rather, it is crafted to align thought and action toward a common goal—the magnet to the paper clip.

### How a Position Statement Comes to Life

A position statement is a critical component of business growth. It is a written summation of what a business is and a rudder for what it wants to be. But, without implementation, a position statement has limitations—like a schooner without wind.

Here's where position players come in, whether they are VPs, directors of marketing, receptionists or mail clerks. Position players can be high-level executives, but they can also be individuals in any tier of your business, no matter what title they hold. They are company ambassadors who, by authentic example, embody your position statement in word and deed—consistently, effortlessly and with integrity.

Take time to recognize these people. They don't drink the Kool-Aid®, they are the Kool–Aid®. They are key players in your quest to succeed.

### Why Position Players Are Viral

With every successful accomplishment, the brain releases dopamine, which delivers a chemical rush similar to the one after a snort of cocaine. The brain remembers the reward and what it did to get it. Anticipation of future reward continues to trip the circuits that flood the brain with happy hormones. The brain then wants more, so the body complies. This "brain candy phenonemon" explains why the right people in an ideal role will thrive there and perform well, again and again, which in turn, makes for good business.

Better yet, position players share the buzz, by default—and fast.

**Researchers at the University of Leeds discovered that only 5% of a crowd can influence its direction, and that the other 95% follow suit without realizing it.** Professor Jens Krause and his PhD student John Dyer conducted experiments in which they directed a group of people to walk around a large hall. They asked them to stay within arms' length of each other, remain silent and refrain from gesturing to communicate. Within the group, they instructed a few individuals to navigate the room in a snake-like, single-file line. In every case, the crowd swiftly followed the path of the "plants" without consulting each other. The researchers concluded that a small percentage of a group is enough to influence its direction. Further, they determined that the larger a group, the less influencers were necessary to affect change. If your business has 20 employees, then 1 person can impact the entire organization, for better or worse.

### Toss the Bad Apples Quickly (But Gently)

Remember the magnet/paper clip experiment? If you strike one of the paper clips of the chain with a hammer, its magnetic quality disappears.

Why?

The strike destroys the alignment of the individual magnetic fields of its particles. Now, the fields neutralize each other, and the paper clip loses its ability to sustain the connection.

And so it is with positioning and position players. One bad apple —the new guy who wants to take you in another direction or operates with an agenda counter to your product or companys' position, can spoil the bunch and cause ripple effects inside your organization and confusion in the marketplace.

It is critically important to have alignment among all your team members, especially among key decision makers and the ability to sustain it. Never underestimate the value in everyone having a clear understanding of your brand, know how to speak about it, and most of all, how to live it. It is your anthem!

A negative Position player can rapidly affect those around them, internally and in your marketplace. Bad vibes, a sour attitude, a dismissive eye roll and an impatient sigh can trigger the release of cortisol, the stress hormone. Like a hammer to a magnetized paper clip, they can incite fear, spike resentment or destroy connections—in an instant.

Oppositely, a positive player with a warm smile, an open mind, a keen listener with a note of gratitude can trigger the release of oxytocin, the bonding hormone. They can boost morale, build cohesion and deepen relationships.

Unfortunately, cortisol has muscles and staying power. It is metabolized far more slowly than oxytocin. As a result, the moment anyone in your business shows signs of negativity—position players in particular because they are powerful influencers—you must take steps to halt "infection" immediately.

**Use your brain—literally—to compel unity.**

Whatever you put out there—whether you can see it or not—sets the tone for conversations and behaviors that follow, in your business and among your customers.

All the more reason to make sure your brand position is authentic. Your advocates will line up in support.

In every interaction and with every communication, lead with warmth, empathy and kindness. Flood the brains of your business stakeholders and the customers you serve with happy hormones that promote bonding. Making smart use of neuroscience will help preserve your position amidst of sea of competition.

# CHAPTER 8

# The winning formula

EVERY JOB PRESENTS A COMPETITIVE ENVIRONMENT, and every role is played in one. To achieve or at least meet the expectations of that role, you must first understand what you do best and how to use your strengths to excel in that situation.

Why do some people win while others lose? Talent and skillsets play a large role. But we all know people who seem to be loaded with talent and superior skills, yet still have trouble succeeding. And at the same time, we all know people with marginal talent and skill who appear to have what it takes to win.

The difference lies in being multi-dimensional. Talent and skill are one-dimensional. Having them alone is like having your weapon cleaned and loaded without knowing where your target is positioned.

At the start, I recounted the details of my high school team's first win on the gridiron and the importance of knowing our competition. Knowing their strengths, weaknesses and tendencies helped position our team to compete. Still, we could not have won the game if we didn't look inward and work to improve our own skillsets. Working on our own game during the week, we were well prepared to perform as a team at game time.

The best athletes in the world can't reach stardom status by training and practice alone, nor by having a one dimensional game. They do so by knowing their opponents, inside and out. They spend countless hours studying film, analyzing the strategies and tendencies of those they're up against. They come to know the strengths, weaknesses, and signature moves of the competition as well as they know their own. And when the timing is right, they capitalize on opportunities like its second nature.

In my youth, I watched basketball on TV all the time. I witnessed great battles between the New York Knicks teams of the 60s and 70s versus the Boston Celtics. I knew every player: Willis Reed, Dave DeBusschere, Bill Bradley, Dick Barnett, Cazzie Russell, Clyde "the Glide" Frazier, even that lanky guy Phil Jackson. And the Celtics had stars like Bill Russell, Dave Cowens, Phil Havlicek, JoJo White, Paul Westphal, and so many more. These were skilled players who relentlessly worked on their own game to be at their best. Team coaches Red Holzman and Red Auerbach devised game plans that positioned their players to succeed as a team while capitalizing on opponents' weaknesses and tendencies. It was amazing to see the ball move and touch so many hands before one player would launch a pure shot, the best shot, sure to be "all net."

These guys were winners because they knew their competition better than they knew themselves and came prepared to win.

A couple times a season, my Dad would take my brother and I to Madison Square Garden to see these players up close. I remember one night we were grabbing a burger post game in what seemed like an exclusive lounge. How we got in I will never know. Seated around us were Willis, "Dollar" Bill, Dave De, Mike Riordan and stretched out across a booth, Phil Jackson. Who would have thought back then that "lanky Phil Jackson" would go on to be a Hall-of-Fame coach to stars like Michael, Kobe and Shack.

Much the same measure of preparation and positioning to compete and win carried the LA Lakers, with players like Wilt Chamberlain, Elgin Baylor, and Jerry West to multiple championships.

Still, having an exceptional product and positioning doesn't guarantee long-term success, but it sure can set you apart and put you in the arena to compete. I am reminded of the Milwaukee Bucks team of the late 60s into early 70s. This club competed with players like Kareem Abdul-Jabbar and Oscar Robertson, unquestionably two of the finest players of all time. Together, they helped their Bucks team capture just one championship in 1971. In later years, Kareem would go on the capture multiple championships with the "Showtime" LA Lakers.

The lessons learned from my High School football experience and those taken from watching the best in NBA competition helped me carry forward the impact of player positioning to my profession.

In the branding arena, knowing your competition is just as critical. Only by understanding the characteristics, behaviors, and identities that comprise your competitive landscape can you hope to discover opportunities for boldly differentiating your brand and position yourself to win.

### Win your customer's mind and heart and claim your piece of the pie.

Look at this another way. Think of a fresh-baked pie. My favorite is blueberry, but for now, imagine a cherry cheesecake pie. Sitting atop the crisp baked crust and rich cheesy blend, there's a sweet mix of "cherry topping." You don't need to claim the whole pie. Others may enjoy the same mix of goodness you do. There's plenty to go around. You're only concerned with carving out your own piece.

To begin, you need two things: the tools to compete and the goods to deliver. If you don't have them, or if you're not sure you do, do the work to improve your product or company.

In other words, prepare. Then define your purpose. Why are you here? Why should people be interested in you?

Next, look inward to assess your attributes and consider how they can help you win.

Finally, take the time to understand your competition.

What you learn from all of these efforts will lead you to that special place where you can stand out; be heard, understood, and appreciated; and compete to win. This is the foundation of work that will reveal to you your own special piece of real estate.

**Congratulations! This is your position.**
**You are now a player. A position player.**

Now it's all about the message, your unique message. The truth of your brand. How well you project it is key. How do you want to project your wonderfulness? What will it look like, smell like, and feel like? What will it stand for? What difference will it make? What can customers expect when they experience your brand? How can you build brand advocates?

Here's my position on how to achieve that:
Stop. Ask. Listen.
Then invite, excite, inform, and entice.
Be sure to spread the word.
That's the winning formula.

82099030R00033